the COLLECTOR'S SERIES *of* TREES

Cedar of Lebanon

SAGE PRESS

Published in 1998

SAGE PRESS,

PO Box Nº 1, Rye, East Sussex TN36 4ZX.

Freephone: 0800 092 33 31

e-mail: summertime @ lineone.net

Set in Palatine italic 9 1/2 on 11 point leading.

Display in Monotype Centaur 48 point.

Design and illustrations

Chris Monk of Yellowduck Design & Illustration.

Research

Claire Clifton and Cindy Stevens

Editor

Cindy Stevens

Series Editor and Publisher

Mrs Bobby Meyer

Printed in Hastings by Judges Ltd

Sage Press would like to thank the Lebanon Tourist and Information Officer, Ministry of Tourism, for their kind contribution and help.

ISBN: 0 - 9531644 - 4 - 6

CEDAR

"COME INTO OUR DWELLING,

in the perfume of the cedars"

(Assyro-Babylonian religious text, 7th century B.C.)

The Cedar of Lebanon appears in many religious texts, including the Bible. Solomon's temple used large supplies of the timber: "all was cedar; there was no stone seen." (1 Kings 6.18) *"The beames of our house are cedars"* (Song of Solomon 1.17)

Cedars were symbols of goodness and strength. "The trees of the Lord are full of sap; the cedars of Lebanon, which he hath planted" (Psalm 104.16).

"His countenance is as Lebanon, excellent as the cedars" (Song of Solomon 5.15).

"The righteous shall flourish like the palm-tree : he shall grow like a cedar in Lebanon" (Psalm 92.12).

Cedars appear in ancient texts concerning the Sumerian hero Gilgamesh. In one story, the sun-god Shamash advises Gilgamesh to fight Khumbaba the Strong, King of the Cedar Mountain. Enlil, the god of the hurricane and master of men's fates, had placed Khumbaba on the mountain to keep its forest of timbers intact, as it was the dwelling of the gods and the sanctuary of the goddess Ishtar.

Gilgamesh manages to defeat Khumbaba, but is forced to flee after Ishtar, spurned in her attempts to seduce the hero, lays a fatal curse on his inseparable companion, Enkidu.

There have been various stories linking the wood of the cedar with the crucifixion of Jesus Christ. It has been said that the cross was made from four different types of wood - palm, cedar, cypress and olive - to signify the four quarters of the globe.

Another tale claims that the upright of the cross was made from cedar wood from a very specific source. Solomon is said to have cut down a cedar tree and buried it where the pool of Bethesda used to stand. A few days before the crucifixion, this cedar reportedly floated to the top of the pool; it was then used for the cross.

Much later, Alphonse Lamartine, the nineteenth century French poet, was inspired to write about the cedars of Lebanon in religious terms :

> *"Sons of the rock, no mortal hand*
> *"Here planted us : God-sown we grew…*
> *"As rafters have our branches dead*
> *"Cover'd the porch of Solomon…*
> *"The beams that form'd the Cross we gave:*
> *"These, red in power of blood to save,*
> *"Were altars of that sacrifice."*

❧ Cedars in Lebanon

In ancient times, forests of cedars and other trees such as cypress covered much of the area. Serious exploitation began in the third millennium BC with the development of the Egyptian timber trade. Assyrians, Persians, Babylonians, all came to extract timber or to demand it in tribute from the coastal towns. The Phoenicians used it in shipping.

By the second century AD, the Roman emperor Hadrian was concerned about the forests and tried to protect them with boundary stones. But the forests continued to disappear. First they were felled for fuel, especially for lime-burning kilns. Then, in medieval times, there was widespread clearance for farmland as well as felling for fuel and construction. The Ottomans destroyed much forest in the nineteenth century, and cedars were felled in the Second World War for use in the building of the Tripoli-Haifa railway.

Today, apart from some isolated clumps growing on inaccessible rocky outcrops, cedars in Lebanon grow chiefly in protected areas. Most famous are the Arz el Rab *(Cedars of the Lord) in Bsharre, many of which are over one thousand years old, exceeding 30 metres in height and 12 metres in girth. They have been protected since 1876, when Queen Victoria financed the building of a high stone wall to keep goats away.*

❧ Cedars in Britain

Although there have been suggestions that its seeds came to Britain with returning Crusaders, it seems likely that the cedar of Lebanon was not introduced into this country until the first half of the seventeenth century. It became much sought after by rich landowners and, later, hoteliers but was rather overtaken by the Indian cedar, or deodar, from the middle of the nineteenth century.

The cedar of Lebanon planted in the grounds of Hart's Hospital, Woodford Green, in 1641 has been claimed as the first planting of the species in Britain. It was still standing in the 1970s, as was one planted five years later at Childrey Rectory, Berkshire, by the then rector and Oxford Professor of Hebrew and Arabic, Dr Edward Pococke.

Another claimant to the title of first British planting was the tree planted in the garden of Tichmarsh Rectory, Northants, allegedly in 1627. A tree in the grounds of Oatlands Park Hotel, Surrey, has also been suggested as the first cedar of Lebanon in Britain. It was planted in the early seventeenth century, reportedly by Prince Henry, son of Charles I.

There are other well-documented examples of cedars being used as individual specimens, as well as being planted in clumps or avenues. In 1970, the tallest tree standing was in the grounds of Petworth House, West Sussex. It towered to 40 metres but was not of great girth. Compared to the cedars at Bsharre, all British specimens have been slender, the broadest being one in Blenheim Park, Oxford, which had a girth of nearly eight metres in 1970.

Daniel Defoe, writing in the first half of the eighteenth century (A Tour Through the Whole Island of Great Britain), *describes the house of the Earl of Burlington, Chiswick House: "On each side are Yew Hedges … in Front of which are planted two rows of Cedars of Libanus, which at present have a fine Effect to the Eye, at a small Distance from the House; for the dark Shade of these solemn ever-green Trees occasions a fine Contraste with the elegant white Building which appears between them."*

At Farnham Castle, Surrey, the seat of bishops for over eight centuries, there are some cedars which were grown from seed brought personally from Lebanon - at the end of the eighteenth century - by Bishop North and his wife.

At Elvaston Castle in Derbyshire, the seat of the Earls of Harrington, six seedlings were planted in the early nineteenth century following major rebuilding works. The then Earl had been given them by Capability Brown as some consolation for Brown's refusal of the commission to landscape the new garden. He had declined the work because "the place is so flat and there is such a want of capability in it."

The poet and artist Edward Lear spent some time in 1860 in seeking out mature specimens in order to complete paintings begun in Lebanon. He found "most magnificent cedars" at Pepperharrow Park and "great and fine cedars" at Paine's Hill, Cobham, Surrey. September saw him working in the gardens of Oatlands Park Hotel, Walton-on-Thames :"Robins singing in the cedar trees. Flies in this room. And hunt thereof."

His biographer, Peter Levi, refers to the "awful drudgery (of) painting cedar trees in the gardens of hotels in

winter".Certainly, Lear does not seem to have been greatly inspired here, and he left the hotel four months later with the work still unfinished.

The word 'Cedars' is often found in the names of houses and roads. Many of these, being late Victorian, will have been named after the deodar, but there are some earlier instances of the cedar of Lebanon being the inspiration for the name.

Literature, too, has its references to garden cedars. In Mrs Gaskell's early Victorian novel Cranford, a visit is made to an elderly bachelor : "We came upon an old cedar tree, which stood at one end of the house -
The cedar spreads his dark green layers of shade."

And there is superstition: in Brethy, Derbyshire, an ancient cedar once belonging to the Caernarvon family is purported to foretell death. If a major branch falls, the death of a family member follows. The last time this happened, Lord Caernarvon did indeed die, following his discovery of Tutankhamun's tomb. The tree is now chained and braced to prevent collapse and so the superstition can no longer be put to the test.

“I BOUGHT FOR BUILDING, MIGHTY cedars, which I cut down with my pure hands on Mount Lebanon” (Nebuchadnezzar).

In its native habitat, the cedar of Lebanon provides admirable timber for construction work and has been much used for buildings and ships.

Buildings

The great size of the cedar made it particularly useful for roofing beams and other parts of buildings where large single pieces of timber were required. Solomon's temple, built with the aid of experts from Tyre, was constructed almost entirely from cedar although its floor was covered with "planks of fir" (1 Kings 6.15).

The Egyptians made great use of cedar. King Snofru (or Sneferu), founder of the Fourth Dynasty, is recorded as having sent 40 trading ships to what is now Lebanon, to fetch cedar and other coniferous logs. Some of the cedar was used to make the doors of the royal palace.

Cedar, possibly from the same shipment, was also used for the beams in the burial chambers of at least one of Snofru's pyramids at Dahshur. They may still be seen in the Southern, or Bent, Pyramid. With its angle of slope changing halfway up, this unique pyramid has two entrances, two galleries and two chambers.

❧ Shipbuilding

Cedar was also in great demand for shipbuilding. Much of the wood obtained by Snofru's expedition was used for this purpose, with three 50 metre ships and various barges being constructed.

A document from the late Twentieth or early Twenty-first Dynasty, The Tale of Wenamun, describes a journey to Byblos to seek cedar wood for shipbuilding and specifically for the construction of a sacred barge for Amon. Thirty baskets of salted fish were taken on the voyage, to serve as partial payment for the timber.

Unfortunately, pirates were waiting for the loaded ships as they left Byblos.

In 1956, archaeologists at Ghiza excavated a 4,600 year old boat-pit. They found a pair of steering oars each well over six metres long and carved from a single piece of cedar of Lebanon.

❧ Other uses

The resin of the cedar is also valuable, and was much used in ancient times. The Egyptians used it in mummification. Pitch made from cedar was used in waterproofing and in caulking boats.

In Britain, its uses have been restricted to the ornamental, as cedar wood is of little practical use when grown outside its native habitat. Although it is easily worked, British-grown cedar is light and spongy, very apt to shrink and warp, and therefore useless for construction. Although cedar wood is much used in the manufacture of good quality garden buildings, this is not from the same tree.

For ornamental purposes, however, cedar was much in demand in British gardens in the seventeenth and eighteenth centuries. Some specimens are well-documented, including those seen by Edward Lear in 1860. The tree at Paine's Hill was once claimed to be the tallest cedar in England.

Art

The cedar of Lebanon, because of its distinctive size and shape, has been popular with artists. It is particularly dramatic when growing, as so often in its native habitat, on mountains and rocky outcrops.

Edward Lear made many sketches in Lebanon in 1858. Writing to Lady Waldegrave, he suggests the cedars as a possible subject for future painting : "There is still a subject of interest - the Lebanon cedars - of which I have got very finished drawings : but the Cedars themselves, very solemn and beautiful as they are - stand alone, and do not include other scenery - so that a picture of the Cedars - will be of the Cedars and nothing else but snow and sheep."

His plans to return to Lebanon in 1860 in order to complete the work were frustrated by fighting between Druze and Christian, and he made no more visits to that country.

A sketch made on his 1858 trip is now in the Victoria and Albert Museum in London.

Common name:
Cedar of Lebanon

Botanical name:
Cedrus libani

Family: *Pinaceae*

Size: *Can reach 35 metres or more under favourable conditions, but 15 to 25 metres is a more usual height in Britain. Trunk often grows only two to three metres before dividing into a number of stems.*

Leaves: *Evergreen, lasting between three and five years. Found chiefly at the end of branches, on the upper side of the branchlets, they are needle-like, grey-green, growing in tufts arranged spirally around dwarf shoots.*

It is interesting to note that in its native Lebanese habitat up in the mountains, the cedar is very different, both in shape and colour, from the specimens we know in Great Britain.
The tree's foliage is a much brighter green than the very characteristic blue/green in Europe, and despite their great age the trees retain a pronounced triangular outline, whereas the distinctive jagged shape of cedars planted in our large gardens is due to loss of key branches caused by storm and wind damage over the years.

Fruit: *Cones. When mature, they are purplish-brown, three to four inches long and one to two inches across. Younger cones are greyish-green tinged with pink. Covered with resin, they stay on the tree for some years. They are not produced until the tree is at least twenty-five years old; in some cases, not for a hundred years.*

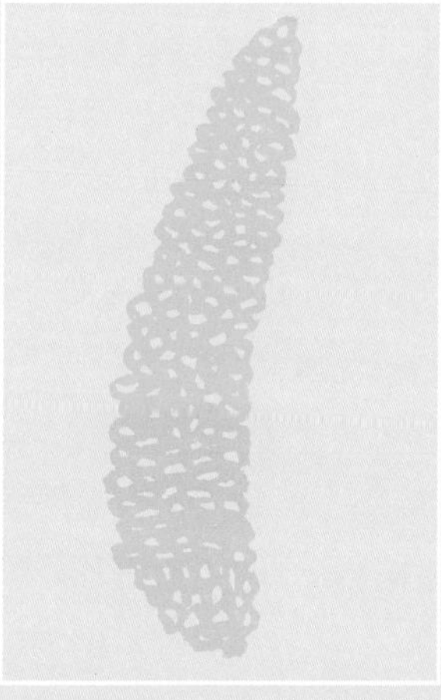

Branches: *Very distinctive, almost horizontal, with branchlets at the ends.*

Bark: *On the trunk, rough, thick and deeply cracked. On the branches, smooth, peeling off in thin flakes.*

Flowers: *Males are upright yellow globes, flowering in September. Females are upright and barrel-shaped, composed of soft green scales.*

otanical Notes

In the same series

Box
Holly
Oak

To be published soon

Ash
Beech
Birch
Catalpa
Elm
Hawthorn
Hornbeam
Monkey Puzzle
Mulberry
Scots Pine
Willow
Yew

If you enjoyed this book and would like
to buy any of the above titles
or require further information
please contact

SAGE PRESS
PO Box Nº 1, Rye, East Sussex TN36 4ZX.
Freephone number: 0800 092 33 31
e-mail: summertime @ lineone.net